NFL Teams

Tennessee Titans

Kenny Abdo

Fly!
An Imprint of Abdo Zoom
abdobooks.com

abdobooks.com

Published by Abdo Zoom, a division of ABDO, P.O. Box 398166, Minneapolis, Minnesota 55439.

Printed in the United States of America, North Mankato, Minnesota.
052021
092021

THIS BOOK CONTAINS RECYCLED MATERIALS

Photo Credits: AP Images, Getty Images, iStock, Shutterstock PREMIER
Production Contributors: Kenny Abdo, Jennie Forsberg, Grace Hansen
Design Contributors: Candice Keimig, Neil Klinepier

Library of Congress Control Number: 2020919509

Publisher's Cataloging-in-Publication Data

Names: Abdo, Kenny, author.
Title: Tennessee Titans / by Kenny Abdo
Description: Minneapolis, Minnesota : Abdo Zoom, 2022 | Series: NFL teams | Includes online resources and index.
Identifiers: ISBN 9781098224813 (lib. bdg.) | ISBN 9781098225759 (ebook) | ISBN 9781098226220 (Read-to-Me ebook)
Subjects: LCSH: Tennessee Titans (Football team)--Juvenile literature. | National Football League--Juvenile literature. | Football teams--Juvenile literature. | American football--Juvenile literature. | Professional sports--Juvenile literature.
Classification: DDC 796.33264--dc23

TABLE OF CONTENTS

TENNESSEE TITANS

On their journey from Houston to Nashville, the Tennessee Titans have displayed giant talent on the football field.

For more than six decades, the Titans have made many playoff appearances and have had future Hall of Famers on the roster!

TITANS
TITANS

KICK OFF

The team began playing in 1960 as the Houston Oilers. They were one of the first teams in the American Football League (AFL).

At first, the Oilers were very successful. They won the AFL **championships** against the Chargers in the 1960 and 1961 seasons!

The team made it to the conference **championship** in both the 1978 and 1979 seasons. Sadly, the Oilers lost both games to the Pittsburgh Steelers.

TEAM RECAPS

TITANS
RAMS
24
3 TIME OUTS 0
21
DOWN
TO GO
BALL ON
QTR
1
10
20
4
TITANS

The team moved from Texas to Tennessee in 1997. They played two seasons as the Tennessee Oilers. In 1999, the team again changed names. Now they'd be known as the Titans!

The 1999 season led to a **Wild Card** game that ended with the "Music City Miracle". The Titans were down by 1 with 16 seconds left. They scored a touchdown from a kickoff return to win the game! The Titans made it to the **Super Bowl** and lost to the Rams 23–16.

Following the 2017 season, the Titans made it back to the playoffs after a 7 year drought. The 2018 season brought more great things. Derrick Henry tied the longest rushing touchdown of all time with a 99-yard run!

TITANS
22

TITANS
17

The Titans ended the 2019 season strong, winning both **Wild Card** and **Divisional** Playoffs. However, they lost the **AFC Championship** to the Chiefs 35–24.

During the 2020 season, the Titans earned their first double-digit winning record and **division** title since 2008. They placed first in **AFC** South but lost the **Wild Card** Playoffs to the Ravens.

TITANS
11

HALL OF FAME

When defensive end Elvin Bethea retired, he held three team records. They were most seasons played (16), most career regular-season games played (210), and most regular-season games played in a row (135). Bethea was **inducted** into the Pro Football Hall of Fame in 2003.

Offensive lineman Bruce Matthews spent his entire career with the Titans, playing in 296 games. That was an NFL record! He played in the Pro Bowl 14 years in a row, another record. Matthews joined the Pro Football Hall of Fame in 2007 and his number 74 is retired by the Titans.

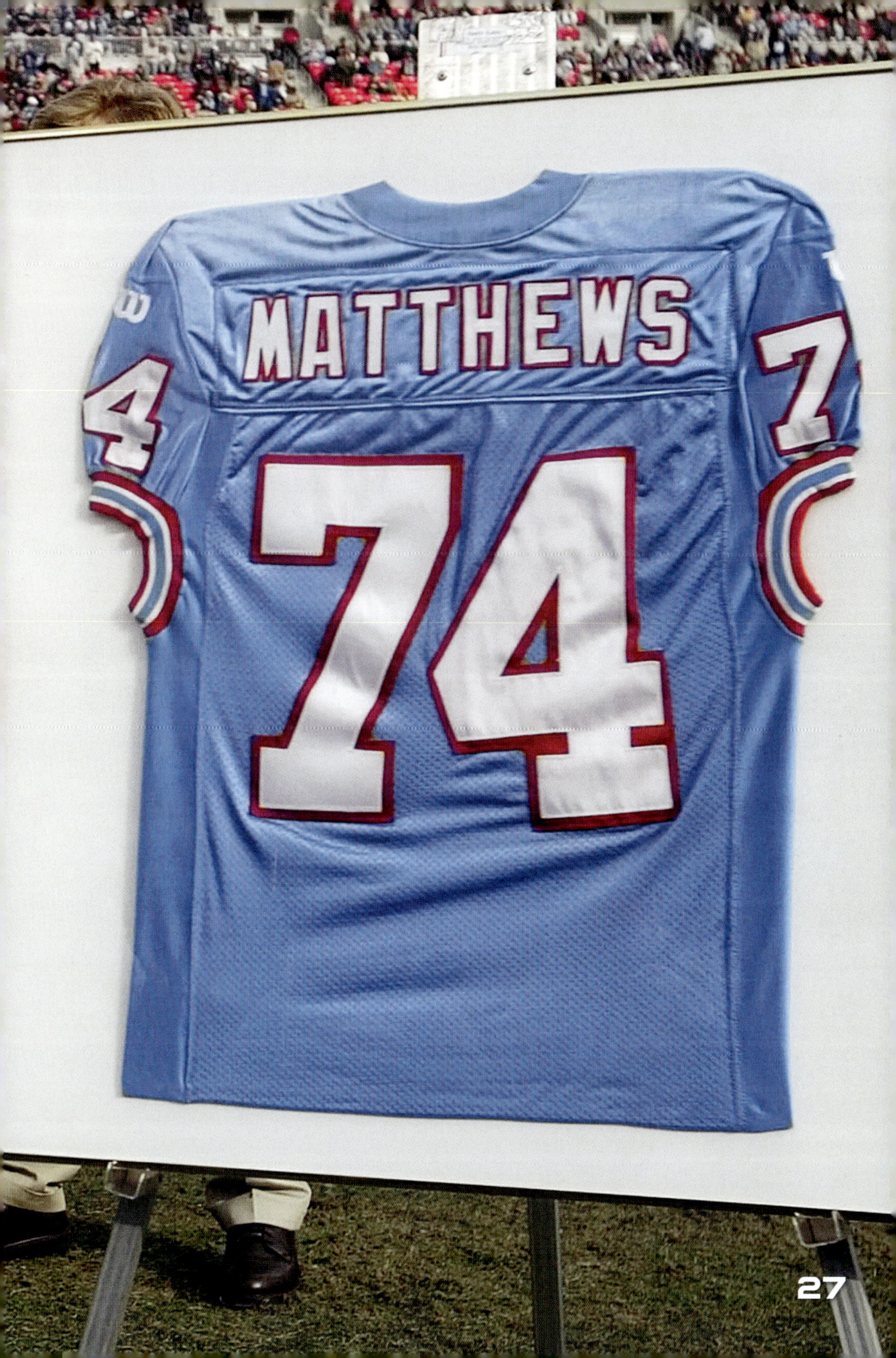
MATTHEWS
74

Warren Moon was one of the most successful **quarterbacks** in NFL history. He set many NFL passing records during his ten seasons with the Titans. In 2006, Moon became the first Black QB **inducted** into the Pro Football Hall of Fame.

GLOSSARY

American Football Conference (AFC) – one of two major conferences of the NFL. Each conference contains 16 teams split into four divisions. The winner of the AFC championship plays the NFC winner at the Super Bowl.

championship – a game held to find a first-place winner.

division – a group of teams who compete against each other for a championship.

induct – to admit someone as a member of an organization.

quarterback (QB) – the player on the offensive team that directs teammates in their play.

Super Bowl – the NFL championship game, played once a year.

Wild Card Round – the first round of the playoffs. Each of the two conferences send four division champions and three wild-card teams to its postseason.

ONLINE RESOURCES

Booklinks
NONFICTION NETWORK
FREE! ONLINE NONFICTION RESOURCES

To learn more about the Tennessee Titans, please visit **abdobooklinks.com** or scan this QR code. These links are routinely monitored and updated to provide the most current information available.

INDEX